# Cookin'

## With

# Moonshine

# DEDICATED TO

My mountain Mama who taught
me a thing or two about how to get
around in the kitchen and the old cook
stove and sharing the gift of laughter.

Thank you kindly.

# INDEX

## Preface

If some of your menfolk kin's got 'em a jug of moonshine, it'd be a good idea to confiscate some of it to use for fixin's for the best eats you can imagine.

Moonshine has its own little kick it can give to dishes, ranging all the way from iced tea to pecan pie.

If you come from a preacher family where moonshine is unavailable, or if you live in a city, you'll find that vodka will work jus' fine with these recipes.

And, these recipes are for making eats tor the grownups. Be sure to fix something else for the little ones; don't jus' leave 'em out scroungin' around like a dog's gotta do.

Now, these recipes call for spring water, but city water will do in a pinch.

# INTRODUCTION

## COOKING MOONSHINE STYLE

I figured some of ya'll would like a little history regarding this mysterious whiskey that we've all seen a movie or two about as well as songs written for it and that will be about as close as we will ever come in contact with it.

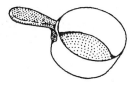

These recipes all call for moonshine but can and should be made with vodka. Moonshine has been given many names; Corn Liquor, Mountain Dew, White Lighting, Kickapoo, Hillbilly Pop, Happy Sally, and possibly others, but we will stick with calling it Moonshine. This homemade whiskey has been around since the first settlers came about and was legal until after the Civil War. For the most part I'd say many a settler made his own brew and it was a part of their everyday lives as well as income for mountain folks where there were little economic choices. The whiskey was dubbed Moonshine because it was made in secret with only the moon for light.

The government began taxing alcohol, then thereafter was the temperance movement.

I read somewhere the concerns about shine that it could possibly contain impurities and toxins that could be harmful from improper brewing. So cooks, I'd say vodka is a good substitute and let the moonshine live on only in stories and tall tales and the stretch of a writer's pure imagination. My Granny would say, she doesn't know all about this here story telling stuff, she only knows that when she went out to the barn to milk her prize cow, Effie, she found a little brown jug with contents that sure seemed to make grown ups happy when she commenced cooking with it's inners. That's her story and she's sticking with it! From her kitchen to yours, I say, ya'll have a good time, and a giggle or two while paging through Cooking Moonshine Style.

# Toddy for the Body

# INDEX

## Moonshine Sippers

½ jigger of moonshine
lemon or lime scrapings (city folks call it zest)
½ ounce lime juice
pure white cane sugar (use enough to take out the burn)
crushed ice
1 ounce sweet & sour mix

Put all ingredients in a shaker and pour into a half pint
jar, but if you want to fancy it up serve it in a martini
glass, either way is fine but remember this is sipping not
gulping. And don't be rocking on the front porch while
sipping, it tends to make your head twirl around.

## Appalachian Ridge Runner Julep

4 fresh mint sprigs     ½-1 ounce moonshine
1 tsp. powdered sugar     2 tsps. cold spring water
crushed ice

Crumple the mint (city cooks call it bruising but that sounds harsh) into a small bowl. Dissolve the powdered sugar and water. Add the moonshine and ice over the mint. Chill for a spell in the icebox and pour through a sieve into a short glass or what ever ya'll are accustomed to drinking from. You can substitute city water for spring water in a pinch. Add a fresh piece of mint. Worth making.

To make this really special, take your flip flops off or your hunting boots and sit with your feet up on a hassock in a cool shady place in the parlor so you can experience the southern ridge runner tingling all the way to your toes. If you're not acquainted with the term ridge runner then let me explain. A true ridge runner is from the Appalachians and we were taught as babies to balance ourselves and walk sort of sideways as we go up around hills so as not to fall off the mountains. Even our farm animals have mastered this walk.

# Mountain Valley Lemonade

12 lemons squeezed      4 or 5 steeped tea bags
1 orange sliced thin       1 cup boiling water
1 cup pure white cane sugar  2 quarts spring water
¼ cup moonshine (a tad more can be used but only a
tad). Use a crock pot, or whatever moonshine want burn
a hole in and have an extra lemon sliced.

Lay your tea bags in the crock pot and pour the hot water
over and let steep for a short spell. Remove the tea bags.
Add the sugar and 2 quarts water leaving about two
inches from the top. Slide in the oranges and lemons.
Swirl it around. Carefully add the moonshine (remember
this is a powerful ingredient). Simmer around about
three hours and time it so as not to interfere with you're
soap operas coming on. Cool and store in icebox until
serving time. Serve over ice. You can use more sugar if
you like it sweeter.

If this is for a hoedown, make sure there are two of you
tending the punchbowl. One to serve and the other to be
lookout for the revenuers. I now understand why a
crock pot is called crocked. Peek inside!

## Spring Tea for the Ladies Garden Auxiliary

| | |
|---|---|
| 1 cup pure cane sugar | 3 cups spring water |
| 5 cups cranberry juice | 2 cups orange juice |
| 1 large can sliced pineapple | 2 liter ginger ale |
| moonshine to taste | 4 black pekoe teabags |

Boil sugar and water until dissolved and steep the teabags in it.  Cool and put into a punchbowl.  Add cranberry and orange juice; add slowly the ginger ale (you may not need all of this) and juice from the canned pineapple. Stir gently and fold in the moonshine.  Add pineapple slices to the punchbowl for decoration, chill until ready to serve.  A little naughty but tasty!

Ladies, this is to be a refreshing beverage with our little repast and the tea is to be sipped from proper frosted glasses, and not guzzled like you see some yahoos do at tractor pulls.  Remember ya'll have choir practice tonight.

# Holiday Punch Mountain Style

| | |
|---|---|
| 3 cinnamon sticks | ½ tsp. allspice |
| 1 ½ qt. apple cider (chilled) | ¼ cup brown sugar |
| 1 ½ qt. cranberry juice (chilled) | 3 oranges sliced |
| 1- 2 (1 liter) bottles ginger ale (chilled) | |
| ¼ cup moonshine chilled (may increase to ½ cup) | |

In a large bowl dissolve the brown sugar in the apple cider. Add all the other ingredients except the moonshine. Blend in the moonshine gently. Return to ice box until ready to serve.

If you're not accustomed to the effects of moonshine then don't embarrass yourselves by adding a full cup and acting like you aint got no sense. Notice I say gently; it has not been proven to my satisfaction that moonshine want explode if agitated; you could loose your eyebrows or scorch your hair. So be gentle for goodness sake.

# Sipping Granny's Eggnog

6 beaten brown shell eggs
2 cups fresh sweet milk
2 more T. sugar
4-5 T. moonshine

1/3 cup pure cane sugar
1 tsp. vanilla extract
1 cup whipping cream
ground nutmeg

In a heavy pot mix eggs, milk and sugar. Cook and stir over medium heat till mixture coats a metal spoon. Then put the pot in the sink that is filled with ice water stirring every couple minutes. Gently add the moonshine and vanilla. Chill 6 to 24 hours. Right before setting out on the dining room table; whip the cream with the 2 tablespoons sugar. Fold into the chilled mixture and sprinkle with nutmeg. Yummy!

Both the men and women run to Granny's eggnog bowl like a herd of stampeding longhorns. They have been known to draw straws to see who would have the pleasure of licking the empty bowl. Ah, what memories of holidays past. One sure fire way of telling who has had their limit is by the redness of their nose and the glow that permeates from their face. Like a light bulb.

# Iced Tea with Moonshine

5-6 tea bags                    1 T. moonshine
¼ cup pure cane sugar           1 whole lemon sliced
2 quarts spring water           ice cubes

Steep tea bags in one quart of boiling water.  Cool down
and add sugar and moonshine.  Pour into container and
add the remaining quart of water and sliced lemons.
You can add more sugar.  Serve over ice.

# Orange Juice with a Kick

1 quart orange juice            2 oranges sliced
1 T. moonshine                  2 T. mountain honey

Mix juice, moonshine and honey into pitcher.  Add the
orange slices.

These two are quick to fix but they do have a punch.
They could even make your mouth numb for awhile.
Maybe you should set a spell until the feeling returns.

## Hot Cocoa with a Moonshine Sting

½ cup pure cane sugar
¼ cup cocoa
pinch of salt
1-2 T. moonshine
1 tsp. vanilla extract

1/3 cup spring water
3 cups sweet milk
1 cup heavy cream
shakes of cinnamon
whip cream

Mix the sugar, cocoa, and salt in a heavy saucepan; stir in the water. Cook until it comes to a boil and stir for a minute. Stir in milk and heavy cream and heat only. Remove from the heat and add the moonshine and vanilla. Serve in deep cups with whip cream and a sprinkle of cinnamon on top.

Granny says, that the only reason Pappy gets out of his rocking chair on a cold day is to go hunting game. He knows she will have a pot of moonshine cocoa waiting for him when he returns. It's odd how Pappy never brings home any game, but how much outside hunting can he get done when he's inside playing checkers at the feed store? I guess checkers could be called game!

## Strawberry Banana Moonshine Slush

1 banana                              1 cup strawberries
1 tsp. mountain honey          ½ T. moonshine
½ cup ice cubes

Put all ingredients into blender and puree. Serve in chilled glass or mug. One serving.


## Berry Moonshine Slush

½ cup raspberries                1 cup blueberries
1 tsp.mountain honey          ½ T. moonshine
½ cup ice cubes

Put all ingredients into blender and puree. Serve in chilled glass or mug. One serving.


## Peach Moonshine Slush

1 ½ cup peaches peeled chopped   ½ -1 T. moonshine
1 T. mountain honey          1 cup ice cubes
½ cup peach nectar

Put all ingredients into blender and puree. Serve in chilled glass or mug. Two evening porch sipper drinks.

## Pineapple Moonshine Cocktail

| | |
|---|---|
| 4 cups fresh pineapple juice | 2 cups crushed ice |
| 2 T. moonshine | 2-3 T. honey |
| 2 slices pineapple | 1 cup lemon lime soda |
| powdered sugar | sieve |

Dip the rims of 4 small glasses or your jelly jars in the powdered sugar and set aside. Slice the two pineapple slices in half and lay them in bottom of glasses. Mix the pineapple juice, honey and lime soda, then add the moonshine and gently blend. Put crushed ice in sieve and position over a bowl. Pour the drink over the ice and into the bowl. Pour the cocktail in the sugared glasses.

A Pineapple Moonshine Cocktail should always be sipped. If you were to drink it down in one gulp your backside might be saying hello to the floor! MODERATION! That's the key.

## MOONSHINE PARTY FOODS

I have noticed on more than one occasion how showers and weddings seem to almost duplicate themselves.  There are cheese trays, fruit trays, vegetable trays, deli trays, cracker trays, fruit punch, salted nuts and a slice of cake which is usually white with some type of colored frosting on it. My observation is from attending these functions on yearly and sometimes monthly basis.  I'm not saying this is a bad thing.  What I'm saying is that it is boring, and we have gotten ourselves in a rut.  We all do it, even I have done it but it is now time to dismiss the old way and get a hitch in our get along and go back to the real food with spark and excitement.

A special gala the men folk don't mind dressing up for or be encouraged to escort you to, something they too enjoy attending, and there is only one way I know of that will get their attention.  Tell them the food has moonshine and I can almost guarantee they'll be in the car before you can get your coat on with the motor running, laying on the horn hollering out the window, "Honey Bun, don't want to be late".

Once ya'll have arrived and the two of you are standing in the buffet serving line, the reason becomes evident to everyone in attendance as to how you got him out of his red plaid shirt, khaki pants and hunting boots and into a suit to come, and it aint a pretty sight; you can't stop this train from derailing. This man is on a mission, he is a diehard lover of moonshine cuisine. He then holds out his plate, with napkin tucked neatly under his chin and his fork positioned in attack mode and very calmly blurts out to the host. "Fill her up".

# Appetizers

# INDEX

## Moonshine Blue Cheese Ball

½ cup Blue cheese          1-2 T. Moonshine
½ cup cream cheese          1 T. minced creasy greens
½ cup toasted and crushed scaley bark nuts

You may not be privileged to have crissy greens or scaley bark nuts. Ya'll can substitute with parsley and walnuts. Mix all ingredients and form a ball and roll it around in the scaley bark nuts, cover with wax paper and put in your icebox.

WARNING! Moonshine cheese balls must be kept in the icebox until ready for the social. Nothing can ruin a hostess reputation faster in these parts than having just one of her little old moonshine cheese balls to spoil and accidentally be served. A visitation to the emergency room by just one guest for their stomach pumping services can off set your social calendar for an entire year.

# Aunt Bipp's Cheese Spread

½ cup cream cheese          1 T. moonshine
1 tsp. chopped kale greens    1 tsp. dried dill
1 T. chopped creasy greens     ¼ tsp dried hot pepper
1 stalk celery (washed and cut into serving size)

Cream cheese should be softened and then put all the
ingrediants except the celery in a bowl and mix with a
fork; spread onto the celery and arrange on a dolly lined
tray.  Green bell pepper or parsley may be substituted for
the kale or crissy greens.

Make a double batch. The ladies have a powerful
appetite for Aunt Bipp's cheese spread and they do get
happy.  The Parson called me after his wife returned
home from one of our ladies club meetings and he said
she was acting strange and then inquired what had I
served?  I replied, "Just cheese, spread onto some little
old celery".  She has not returned to my house for
another club meeting.

## Old Hickory Ham Moonshine Ball

2 T. melted butter            2 T. moonshine
1 T. chopped green onions     1 T. red bell pepper
½ cup snipped creasy greens   1-3oz. pkg. cream cheese
1 cup shredded hard cheese    1 cup minced cooked ham
2 dashes of hot sauce
Enough crushed hickory or walnuts nuts to cover the ball

Mix all ingredients except nuts in a bowl and form a
ball; roll the ball around in the nuts. Wrap in wax paper
and store in the icebox. May substitute parsley for crissy
greens.

This is one cheese ball that the hunters cotton to. Have
you ever thought why hot sauce, moonshine and hunters
go together like fresh churned butter on hot cornbread?
I have no explanation for this phenomenon. It is what it
is.

# Stuffed Moonshine Tommy Toes

1 8oz. cream cheese
1 T. sweet milk
1-2 T. moonshine
24-26 tommy toes

1 T. snipped chives
¼ tsp. minced garlic
1 tsp. minced onion

Cut the tops off the tommy toe tomatoes (or cherry tomatoes) and spoon out the seeds, turn upside down to dry on a paper towel. Meanwhile put all the other ingredients in a bowl and mix thoroughly. With a small spoon fill each of the tommy toes.

I realize some of ya'll are not privileged to have the ingredients I stock in my kitchen pantry, icebox or root cellar and must substitute. Check your barns and see if there is some old jug that your great -great grand pappy may have forgotten about. On these special occasions my cousin, Wilbur, who is known in the mountains as a human bloodhound can detect an old forgotten moonshine jug by sticking his nose up in the air or on the ground. His hound dog, Bo, comes in a close second. Talented pair.

## Moonshine Mustard Glazed Pork Ribs

½ cup dark brown sugar
¼ cup chopped onion
½ tsp. chopped garlic
2 ½ - 3 lbs. cut up spare ribs

½ tsp. hot sauce
¼ cup mustard
2 T. mountain honey
¼ cup moonshine

Rub the sugar into the ribs and let set while the cook stove gets up to 350 degrees. Lay the ribs on a foil lined cookie sheet with a rim and roast for about one hour. Meantime in a small heavy cooking pot, put all the other ingredients and cook until heated through. Move the pot off the burner. Brush just a little on the pork ribs and bake another thirty minutes. Reheat the left over sauce and pour into a bowl for added dipping.

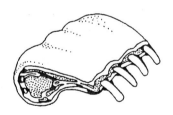

I'm sure if a young lady seeking the right young man for marrying purposes should prepare these tantalizing moonshine ribs it would enhance her chances with eligible beaus to choose from. Much like putting vanilla extract behind your earlobes. Gentlemen seem to be attracted to anything that reminds them of moonshine, groceries, or bass fishing.

## June Bugs Moonshine Crab Salad

2 shakes of hot sauce
½ cup chopped celery
2 -3 T. real mayonnaise
1 tsp. celery seed
2 tsp. lemon juice

½ cup chopped green onions
1 lb. fresh crab
fresh ground pepper
2 T. moonshine
salt to taste

Chop crab meat and place in bowl sprinkled with lemon juice, add the other ingredients and toss gently. Store covered in icebox until ready to serve. This is not to be gooey, so add one tablespoon of mayonnaise at a time.

A hostess would be mighty proud to have June Bug's crab salad sitting on her buffet table along side the pickled hog feet, fried fat back biscuit sandwiches and sweet iced tea. Makes you hungry thinking about it.

# Moon Shining Chicken Wings

20 chicken wings
2 T. hot sauce
1 ½ cup catsup
2 T. moonshine

2 tsp. lime juice
4 T. mountain honey
3 T. melted butter

Mix all the ingredients in a dish; add the wings (snip off the tips) cover and let sit about 30 minutes in the icebox. Preheat oven to 350. Put wings in a single layer on a foiled lined long rimmed baking sheet and bake about 1 hour.

For years we have enjoyed an annual moonshine chicken wing eating contest here in the mountains. And every year after the contest someone driving back down the mountain is stopped by a patrolman and given a sobriety test to see if they're under the influence of moonshine wings, and if caught with an open bag of wings, they could be spending time in the county pokey. Alcohol is alcohol if you're drinking it or eating it! BEWARE!

## Shrimp Dripping In Moonshine Sauce

| | |
|---|---|
| 1 cup catsup | 2 T. lemon juice |
| 2 T. moonshine | 1 T. mountain honey |
| 1 chopped green onion | salt and pepper |
| 1 lb. boiled shrimp (chill in icebox) | |

Mix all the other ingredients; pour into bowl and cover and store in the icebox with the shrimp until ready to eat. I like to add all the shrimp to the sauce and swish them around. Saves time with your little toothpick stabbing at the buffet table.

SAFETY ALERT. While preparing moonshine recipes in your kitchen don't forget to check the drip pan underneath the icebox. It can spill out onto your linoleum, causing you to slip and fall. It would be difficult explaining to the ambulance driver as your being toted to the hospital that because you reek of moonshine is not at all the reason why you fell and broke your foot. I get the vapors thinking about it.

## Chicken Salad with a Twang

| | |
|---|---|
| 3 T. mayonnaise | 2 T. chopped green onion |
| ½ cup chopped celery | 1 T. moonshine |
| 2 T. chopped nuts | salt and pepper to taste |
| 3 cups chopped cooked chilled chicken | |
| 1 tsp celery seed | |

Mix all your ingredients and store in a sealed bowl in the icebox. May add more mayonnaise to make it creamy.

Pappy was heading to town on errands and Granny told him that as long as he was going he could also fetch something she needed. Returning home Pappy handed her a jar of mayonnaise. Granny glared at him and said. "I didn't ask for mayonnaise, I said get bandaids!" Either way, Granny's moonshine cooking has pickled Pappy's brain, or the sixty years of marriage. Pappy got his marching orders to scat back down to the store.

# Moonshine Sausages

| | |
|---|---|
| 2 pkgs. cocktail sausages | 3 cups catsup |
| 1 cup mountain honey | 3 shakes hot sauce |
| 3-4 T. moonshine | crock pot |

Mix honey, catsup and hot sauce in crock pot. Add the sausages and put the setting on low. Right before you put them in a dish add the moonshine and let sit in the warm sauce about twenty minutes.

Have ya'll noticed how cooking with moonshine takes less amount of alcohol than other liquors? The reason is simple enough. It's POTENT to the last drop, no matter how old it gets. Moonshine just want die. It isn't like other alcohol that goes flat, stale, evaporates or turns to vinegar. Sort of strange. Ya'll be careful; it's stronger than we are. I think it has a mind of its own.

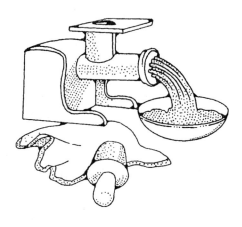

## Corned Beef Roll-Ups with Hot Fixins'

| | |
|---|---|
| 1 lb. deli sliced thin corned beef | 1 T. horseradish |
| 1 lb. deli sliced thin Swiss cheese | ½ cup mayonnaise |
| 1 T. moonshine | toothpicks |
| fresh ground black pepper to taste | |

Mix the horseradish, mayonnaise, pepper and moonshine in a small bowl and set aside while you unroll the corned beef and swiss cheese onto wax paper. Take one slice corn beef and spread with mixture, and then lay a slice of swiss cheese and roll it up. Cut in half and pierce through with a toothpick until all have been rolled up. Store them in a long plastic dish with a sealed lid. Place in icebox until ready to be served. You may use mustard in place of the mayonnaise but it will be spicier.

These little roll-ups are simple and have that bite the men folk like because they tend to bite back.

## Smoked Peppered Turkey and Peppered Ham Bites

| | |
|---|---|
| 2 packages med. flour tortilla shells | 1 cup hot mustard |
| 1 lb. deli thin smoked turkey | 1 T. moonshine |
| 1 lb. deli thin smoked ham | 1 T. brown sugar |
| shredded lettuce | 2 bell peppers |

In a small bowl mix the mustard, moonshine and brown sugar and set aside. Shred head lettuce fine. Slice bell peppers (red and green) in thin strips and drain on paper towel. For each flour shell spread a small amount of the sauce then a couple slices each of turkey and ham; sprinkle with lettuce and lay a few strips of bell pepper. Roll up and slice across either two or three times. Pierce with toothpicks to hold together. Make more sauce if needed.

You don't need to work yourselves to death to be a good host or hostess. Keep it simple. Just make plenty so you can be with your guests instead of running back and forth to the icebox. You don't want to miss out on any new gossip.

## DOUSING VEGETABLES

I can remember as a child, my Mama stressed the importance to eat all our vegetables so we would grow big and strong. She was right. But one thing my Mama didn't stress, was adults like a little more fire cooked in them. So this is devoted to what Mama didn't tell me. How much tastier a bowl of poke salad greens, or even creasy greens are with just a touch of moonshine, and this is how a lady found out long ago how the two compliment each other. It seems a lady accidentally knocked the little brown jug over and splashes went into a pot of creasy greens she had cooked. Not to mention the moonshine spilled down onto the floor scorching her new linoleum. She was thankful the stove wasn't turned on or she might have had the Mountain Holler volunteer fire truck visiting outside her kitchen door. I can all but visualize the newspaper headlines in the Mountain Holler Gazette.

A mountain woman's kitchen burns to the ground as did her pot of creasy greens by a fire of unknown origin. Reports of an odd but tantalizing aroma was detected mingled with the smoke and was witnessed by the woman's nosy neighbors. The Mountain Holler firemen had to be revived continually with black coffee to help sober and steady them on their feet as they continued to battle the mouth watering blaze. An investigation will follow once everyone has sobered up.

So cooks, be careful. Never set the moonshine jug anywhere close to the cook stove. The kitchen you save may be your own. Remember ladies, nothing is worth losing a pot of creasy greens.

# Veggies & Side Dishes

# INDEX

## Creasy Greens Doused In Moonshine

2-3 ham hocks                        ¼ bushel creasy greens
moonshine to taste               salt to taste
apple cider vinegar            touch of sugar
small amount of spring water

In the biggest pot you have, start boiling the ham hocks until almost fork tender. Remove the hocks. Wash the creasy greens at least twice in your stainless kitchen sink. Add a little of the greens at a time to the ham hock water simmering on the stove until all the greens are in; add a little salt. Cook until greens are very tender. Cut ham from hocks and add to the greens. In a small container mix the moonshine with a small amount of water, sugar and salt. When you are ready to serve, douse the greens with it.

Don't eat too many at one sitting. You'll know why if you do. You want need a spring tonic. Maybe ya'll need to keep the light on in the outhouse.

## Green Beans and Moonshine Onions

| | |
|---|---|
| 2 lbs. fresh green beans | 2 hot onions sliced |
| 4 slices fatback | 2 tsp. pure cane sugar |
| 1 T. moonshine | salt to taste |
| 1 T. mountain cider vinegar | 2 T. spring water |

Wash and snap your beans. Parboil and rinse. In the same pot add the fatback and beans. Add water to cover and cook until tender, add salt to taste. Meanwhile in a bowl put the moonshine and water; add the salt, sugar and vinegar. Stir around and then add the sliced onions.

I enjoy making and eating onion sandwiches. The only drawback when using this particular recipe is not to go near an open flame for at least one hour after eating. The reason is obvious.

## Ham Bone, Peas, Onions and Moonshine

| | |
|---|---|
| 1 ham bone | 3 cups sweet June peas |
| 1 cooking onion diced | 2 T. moonshine |
| salt to taste | spring water |
| 1 T. flour | |

In a heavy pot put the ham bone with just enough water to cover the bone and cook until you get tired of cooking it. Remove about ½ cup of the liquid and let cool down to mix with the flour and moonshine. Add the June peas and onion. Cook just a few minutes. Remove from burner and then add the flour mixture.

Never waste food. Find a way to reheat leftovers and put them back on the kitchen table day after day. That's where a ham bone and moonshine come in handy. Smelling the ham bone makes the men folk think that there will be meat for supper and the moonshine makes them care less that it aint.

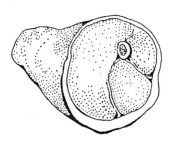

## Root Vegetables with Moonshine Camouflage

| | |
|---|---|
| 2 kohlrabies peeled | 2 parsnips peeled |
| 2 rutabagas peeled | 2 carrots peeled |
| 2 purple turnips peeled | 2 hot onions chopped |
| 4 pats. churned butter | salt & pepper to taste |
| 2 tsp. moonshine | ½ tsp. sugar |
| 6 slices fried breakfast bacon (crumbled) | |

Cut up all the vegetables and put in a pot with water to cover; add the sugar and cook until tender; drain. Add salt, pepper, butter and moonshine; fold. Sprinkle the crumbled bacon on top and serve.

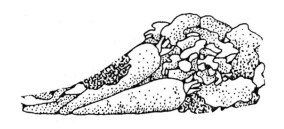

Not everyone likes the taste of strong root vegetables and Granny was asked what where the benefits of cooking and eating them? She answered vitamins. Then Pappy was asked what was the benefit the root vegetables got by adding the moonshine? He answered, camouflage.

## Creamed Turnips and Tasty Moonshine

1-2 lb. turnips
2 slices fat back (salt pork)
salt and sugar to taste

1 T. moonshine
butter to taste

Peel and dice the turnips and put in a pot. Add enough
water to cover. Add the fat back and cook until turnips
are tender. Drain and remove the fatback. Add the
moonshine, butter, salt and sugar. Mash until creamy.
Add another dollop of butter.

People are on more diets than you can imagine. Cousin
Lottie decided to go on the mountain diet. A mountain
of taters, a mountain of butter, and a mountain of
moonshine. Lottie always was the trend setter in my
family; to bad that last mountain got her.

## Squashed Squash

1-2 lb. butternut squash diced          ¼ cup brown sugar
¼ cup butter                            1 tsp. cinnamon
2 T. moonshine                          salt to taste
½ cup vidalia onion chopped

Put squash and vidalia onion in pan and sprinkle with
salt and cover with water.  Stew until tender; drain and
add the butter, sugar, cinnamon and moonshine.  Mash
until creamy.  You may use sweet onions in place of the
vidalia.

Squash is a vegetable that you can stew, fry or eat raw.
With a hint of moonshine in it sure puts a little fire to it.

## Sweet Taters and Moonshine

1-2 T. moonshine                    ½ cup brown sugar
¾ stick melted butter           1 tsp. vanilla extract
2 T. molasses                         6 sweet taters
3 shakes of cinnamon           ½ cup chopped pecans

Boil the sweet taters in their skins until tender. Remove and put them in cold water. After cooled, slice length wise and put in buttered baking dish. Mix the moonshine, melted butter, vanilla and molasses. Dollop and spread over potatoes. Sprinkle brown sugar and pecans. Bake in 325 oven until heated through.

I declare, this is super sweet. Open the kitchen window wide so the smell floats out into the mountain air. Ya'll will have the bees jealous. What a sight!

## Fresh Pickled Okra, Cukes and Onions

1-lb. fresh okra
8-10 green onions
1 clove garlic
½ cup apple cider vinegar
¼ cup spring water

2 med. cucumbers
1 tsp. fresh dill chopped
sugar and salt to taste
1 T. moonshine
¼ cup olive oil

Parboil okra whole for a minute, then plunge the okra in ice water to chill down and drain. Slice cucumbers and put aside in bowl that has a lid. Cut onions in bite size pieces and put into the same bowl. Cut okra in bite size pieces and add to the bowl and all the other ingredients. Swish around and put the lid on and store in the icebox until your ready to eat.

This is good and tasty. Adults like to eat it with everything. You'll know who ate the most because they belch the most. Ah! Another sign of a good cook.

# Moonshine Pickled Beets

3 cans beets
¼ cup mountain vinegar
¼ cup spring water

2 T. moonshine
¼ cup cane sugar
salt to taste

In saucepan add the vinegar, water, beet juice, sugar and salt; heat through. Remove from stove and add the moonshine. Let it get room temperature. Place the beets in a bowl and pour the liquid on and gently swirl the beets; cover tightly and put in the icebox to chill. Hard boiled eggs can be added to the beets for pickled eggs.

I declare, if you are not careful and eat too many, then ya'll be as pickled as the beets.

# Fresh Corn from the Cob

12 ears of corn cut from cob   ½ red bell pepper chopped
½ med. diced hot onion        ½ green bell pepper
½-1 stick melted butter       1-2 T. moonshine
1 T. mountain honey           ½ tsp. salt
½ cup sweet milk              ½ tsp. black pepper

In a small saucepan melt the butter and add the bell
peppers and onion and saute until tender. Remove from
the burner and add the honey. Put the ingredients in a
heavy cooking pot; add the corn, salt and pepper; lastly
add the milk. Cook on low stirring often so as not to
stick. Add the moonshine right before serving.

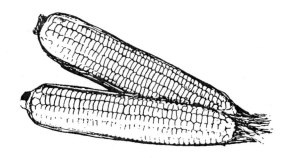

Nothing can make grown-ups hungrier than smelling
corn simmering. I doubt you will need to call your
guests to the dinner table. They'll probably be sitting at
the table waiting for you. Always remember butter is
better.

## Moonshine Cheese Broccoli & Cauliflower

3 cups broccoli florets     3 cups cauliflower florets
1 can pearl onions drained    1/3 stick butter
2 T. moonshine         dash of sugar and salt
¼ cup grated hard cheese    ¼ cup pepper jack cheese
4-5 strips bacon fried and crumbled

Steam the florets until almost fork tender. In a small saucepan melt the butter and fold in the drained pearl onions. Remove from burner. Add the pepper jack cheese, moonshine, salt and pepper. Put the florets in a serving dish and gently add the bacon and cheese mixture; put grated cheese mixture on top.

I think Pappy would like this dish so well he might even consider helping Granny wash the dishes after supper.

## Asparagus and Carrots

| | |
|---|---|
| 1 bunch fresh asparagus | 4 carrots |
| 1/3 cup butter melted | 1 T. fresh dill |
| 1 T. chopped fresh parsley | salt to taste |
| 1 T. moonshine | 1/8 tsp. cane sugar |

Wash and snap the tough ends off the asparagus. Wash and slice the carrots like thin pennies. Put the carrots in the steamer first and lay the asparagus on top. When fork tender remove from burner. Mix the moonshine, melted butter, fresh dill, salt and sugar and pour over the vegetables in a serving dish. Sprinkle the fresh parsley on the top and serve.

This is one of those no fuss dishes. Tastes like ya'll been working steady over it. This would be tasty as a side dish to any entrée. Granny wouldn't say entrée; that would be getting on one's high horse. She would say it goes with anything she says it goes with!

# FRUITS POWERED BY MOONSHINE

Nothing is quite as pleasing to the taste buds as sweet ripened fruit, fresh or dried. Fruit adds to any meal or snack. Fruit is full of vitamins and natural energy and with a little moonshine added in it turns into a power source when used sensibly. Some folks act like fruit is a dose of medicine instead of something good for them and one way to get it down them is with a touch of moonshine. Alcohol and fruit just seem to blend together like flies at an ice cream social. Spiking watermelon or any other fruit can get your attention real quick after the first bite. Some folks who never much cottoned to fruit have all of sudden gotten hankerings for it. I wonder why?

I wouldn't doubt that if you were at a adult gathering and put all types of desserts on one table and fruits touched with moonshine on another table and then told everyone what was in the fruit, you would need to get out of the way as everybody begins running like they were in some sports marathon trying to get to the fruit table first. Feet would be flying not to mention all the pushing and shoving going on. It's hard to believe some of these same folks five minutes earlier acted like they could barely get one foot to go in front of the other. Mind you, they possibly will tell you they really aren't partakers of the moonshine brew and just want to see what it tastes like off the record. I would ask them what record that might be.

So this chapter is for all the folks who just need to be gently reminded fruit comes from a tree, a bush, a plant and from an old fruit jar, ya'll know I'm saying this off the record. SURE!

# Moonshine
# Spiked Fruits

## INDEX

## Peaches Creamed

| | |
|---|---|
| 10 fresh ripened peaches | ½ tsp.lemon juice |
| ½ cup white cane sugar | 2 T. moonshine |
| dash of cinnamon | |

Wash, peel and slice peaches; put in a bowl. Add the lemon juice and sugar. You can add more sugar gradually. Add the moonshine and fold. Set in icebox to chill. Sprinkle cinnamon on when serving.

This goes well with a slice of pound cake or served on top of peach ice cream; or eat as is with plain sugar cookies. I don't think a southerner could ever get enough peaches. We make preserves, syrup, pies, cakes and can. Grandpa Maynard summed it up this way; nothing is as handy as having your own peach tree planted in the front yard and a moonshine jug out in the barn.

# Moonshine Fruit Bowl

| | |
|---|---|
| 1 cantaloupe | 4 cups watermelon |
| 1 pint blueberries | 1 lb. strawberries |
| 1 pint cherries (pitted) | ½ cup pure cane sugar |
| ¼ cup moonshine | ¼ cup spring water |

Mix the moonshine, sugar and water and set aside. Cut up into bite size pieces of the cantaloupe and watermelon and put in large bowl. Half the cherries and put into the bowl. Cut the strawberries in half and add to the bowl. With a spatula gently fold the fruit. Sprinkle the moonshine mix over the fruit and then add the blueberries on the top. Cover and chill in icebox until ready to eat.

Someone once asked Pappy to say the first word that came to mind when they said watermelon. He replied, moonshine. They said cantaloupe. Pappy answered moonshine. Do you think Pappy was thinking about a fruit bowl? Sweet old fellow.

# Stewed Apples

3 tart apples                      3 yellow apples
3 red apples                       ½ stick butter
½ cup brown sugar                  2 shakes of cinnamon
1 shake of cloves                  2 T. moonshine
¼ cup water

Wash and core the apples. Slice thin with peelings on.
In a large heavy skillet melt the butter and put the apples
in. Stir fry until almost tender. Sprinkle in the
cinnamon and cloves and brown sugar. Remove from
burner and with wooden spatula fold and add the water
and then the moonshine. Add more sugar if you have a
sweet tooth.

Stewed apples on a cold day with buttermilk biscuits
will get your heart pumping and your feet stepping
lively. Yummy!

### Blackberry Moonshine Puree

5-6 cups blackberries
2 T. lemon juice
2 T. lime juice

2 T. moonshine
¾ -1 cup pure cane sugar
dash cinnamon

Puree the blackberries in a blender and press the puree through a sieve to catch the seeds. Return to blender and add the lemon and lime juice, moonshine, cinnamon and sugar. You may want more sugar.

This would be tasty over vanilla ice cream, vanilla custard, and even drizzled over baked rice pudding and crepes that have been stuffed with blackberries and sprinkled with powdered sugar. Yummy! We southerners love our blackberries and hunting them through briar patches on a hot July day makes you appreciate every berry. And, if you happen to trip and start tumbling back down a hill with your full pail, the first words from your mouth is not to help me because I'm going over the edge, we say, "YA'LL SAVE MY BERRIES, I CAN WAIT."

# Strawberries Drowning in Moonshine

2 quarts strawberries      1½ cups pure cane sugar
2-3 T. moonshine        ½ T. cornstarch
mint leaves             ½ cup spring water
1 tsp. lemon juice

Wash, cap and cut in half all but 2 cups of the berries to be left whole for later in the recipe; put the halved berries into a separate bowl and add the sugar and mix with a spatula. Add the moonshine and fold a little more. Cover and place in the icebox to chill and make juice overnight. The next day pour most of the juice off the berries into a small saucepan; add the lemon juice. Mix the cornstarch with water and also add to the pan. Cook on medium and stir constantly until slightly thickened and remove from burner. Bring to room temperature and then add to the berries. When serving add the whole berries and a mint sprig on top.

This is great for that added sweet taste you hanker for but not all the calories from a rich dessert. Not to mention that extra buzz that'll come with it. Eat only a small helping. This is white lighting not spring water!

## Moonshine Fruit Bowl

5 passion fruit        1 fresh pineapple cut up
1 cup red seedless grapes    1 cup green grapes
1 cup sweet cherries        sliced almonds
2-3 T. moonshine        1 T. mountain honey
¼ cup warm spring water

Mix the moonshine, honey and warm water in cup and set aside. Slice the passion fruit and lay the slices in a bowl; add all the other fruits and fold. Pour the liquid over the top. Add the nuts on top. Very simple.

I like the easy way of fixing food. Granny would say, it aint so much the time it takes to making a meal, but the joy you get from doing it that counts. Granny is my hero.

## Pineapple, Kiwi and Mangos

2 reg. cans pineapple chunks     6 kiwis sliced
4 mangos sliced     2 T. cane sugar
2 T. moonshine     ½ cup coconut
1 cup glazed pecans

Drain pineapple in measuring cup and add the
moonshine and sugar.  In bowl put the pineapple,
mangos and three of the kiwis.  Fold in the pecans and
coconut. Pour the liquid on and fold.  Add the remaining
three kiwis on top.

If this is being served at a large party, I suggest you keep
an eye out for Maudie.  She does hanker for spiked fruit.
You'll know which lady she is, she's the one camped out
by the buffet table holding onto the fruit bowl.

# Bananas on a Binge

| | |
|---|---|
| 6 bananas | ½ cup brown sugar |
| 1 lemon | ½ stick butter |
| 1 ¼ cup spring water | 1 T. moonshine |
| 1 cup chopped fine walnuts | ½ tsp. vanilla extract |

In a bowl put one cup water and juice from the lemon. Peel the bananas and cut in half and let the twelve pieces sit in the lemon water for thirty seconds. Lay two bananas slices on each dessert dish and sprinkle with nuts. In a small sauce pan melt the butter and add the brown sugar and ¼ cup of water. Cook down for about one to two minutes. You want the syrup to be thin. Remove pan from burner and add the vanilla stirring constantly. Add the moonshine. Dip over the bananas and serve immediately. Serves six.

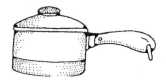

Some folks have a powerful appetite like my Cousin Homer, and he would say this wasn't enough to fill a hollow tooth and then complain it needed more moonshine, of course that's after he has finished off the entire amount!

Cantaloupe Zing

| | |
|---|---|
| ¼ cup mountain honey | 2 T. moonshine |
| ¼ cup water | 1 cup raspberries |

1 large cantaloupe peeled and diced
raspberry sorbet

Dilute the honey, water and moonshine and set aside.
Place the diced cantaloupe in a bowl and add the liquid.
Store covered in icebox to chill. When ready to serve,
spoon out into individual bowls; add a scoop of
raspberry sorbet beside it; sprinkle raspberries on the
fruit and sorbet. Try other fruits for a change.

This sounds tempting to be served for a summer supper.
Some folks think cantaloupe is just for breakfast but I
wouldn't doubt you might catch sight of one or two of
you guests scraping their bowls for that last little taste.

## Citrus and Moonshine

| | |
|---|---|
| 4 oranges peeled, sectioned | 2 T. moonshine |
| 4 tangelos peeled, sectioned | ¼ cup pure cane sugar |
| 2 grapefruit peeled, sectioned | 1 cup orange juice |
| 1 cup pitted sweet cherries | mint sprigs |

Mix moonshine, sugar and orange juice in a bowl and set aside. In large bowl put the oranges, tangelos and grapefruit. Pour liquid over and add the cherries and fold in. Chill covered in the icebox. Serve in bowls with a mint sprig on the side.

This sort of reminds you of a Mint Julep, but instead of drinking it, you're eating it. Take care this is fortified with vitamin C as well as moonshine. Some folks could be getting a double burn when they eat. Tasty!

## HOMEY MOONSHINE SOUPS

There's one thing about soup. You can pitch just about everything in and call it soup. Aunt Sadie said that she pitched everything in but the kitchen sink. Her husband, Uncle Claude, said it tasted like it too! It is true many a leftover has found its way to our stock pots. Aunt Sadie said waste not want not. Uncle remarked that waste was waste no matter how you came by it. Now I'm pretty sure if Aunt Sadie had added a touch of moonshine then Uncle Claude would have slurped it down.

What a wonderful aroma abounds with a kettle of soup simmering. A supper all in one that's satisfying even to someone as cantankerous as Uncle Claude. Soup is welcomed at just about every occasion. Pappy could hardly wait to eat when the soup came to the table. Granny would always caution him to let it cool but Pappy being Pappy couldn't wait and took the first mouthful and burned his mouth and throat. He then would look at Granny and say, "You cooked it to hot."

Cooks, enjoy taking older recipes and adding a spark of something new. Moonshine is the spark. Just a fine touch can possibly add new life to an old recipe. Not only is soup filling but with the moonshine added in it may put you in a sleepy time mode. So you may want to stay close to the couch or recliner after supper.

# Soups

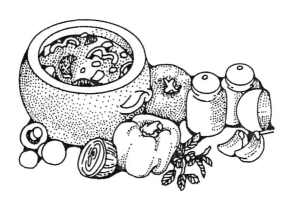

# INDEX

# Tottering Chili

| | |
|---|---|
| 2 lbs. lean ground beef | 2 large onions chopped |
| 1 large can diced tomatoes | 1 small can tomato sauce |
| 1 reg. can kidney beans | 1 reg. can pinto beans |
| 1 reg. can great northern beans | 1 cup water |
| 2-3 T. moonshine | 1 T. chili powder |
| 1 clove garlic | ½ tsp. cayenne |
| crock pot | salt to taste |

Brown ground beef, garlic, and onions. Drain any liquid off and put meat in a crock pot. Drain the beans and add to meat and stir. Add the tomatoes, sauce, water and seasonings. Add the moonshine and stir. Cook on low for about four hours and taste to see if you want to add more seasinings. Add a little more water if you want it thinner. Hot corn bread is good with this.

For most adults it would be servings of six to eight, but if you are hosting a meal for the hunt club they'll probably be out in your kitchen hunting around for more.

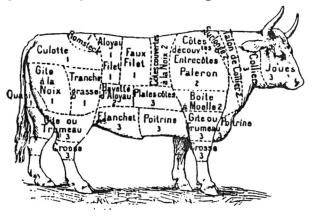

## Vegetable Beef Soup

| | |
|---|---|
| 1 large can tomatoes | 2 bags. frozen soup vegetables |
| 1 large potato diced | 2 stalks celery chopped |
| 1 large onion diced | 1 cup chopped cabbage |
| 6 okra chopped | 1 ½ lbs. stew beef (bite size) |
| 3 T. moonshuine | 3 cups beef broth |
| 2 beef short ribs | 2 turnips chopped |
| salt to taste | |

Set the frozen vegetable bags on the drain board to thaw. Parboil the beef and short ribs in a very large pot; rinse and return to pot. Pour the broth in and cook until starting to get tender. Add the fresh vegetables and stir around. Add the tomatoes and salt. Remove from heat and add the moonshine and stir. Add the thawed vegetables and stir. Start off getting the soup cooking and then lower the heat to about medium low until done.

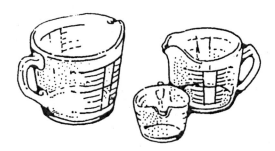

One thing about it, whoever is doing the cooking will be doing a powerful lot of tasting. Too mouth watering to resist. Make sure you have a tee-totaler in the kitchen with you to do the serving and their arm to hang on to as you are being led to the table. Sober up!

## Pumpkin Soup Creamed

3 T. olive oil
1 celery rib diced
1-48oz. chicken broth
2 tsp. fresh chopped tyme
2-3 T. moonshine
½ stick butter

3 carrots diced
1 large onion diced
1 29 oz. canned pumpkin
2 cups heavy cream
nutmeg and salt to taste

In a heavy large pot on medium heat melt butter and cook the carrots, celery and onion until softened. Add the broth, pumpkin and thyme and simmer fifteen minutes. Remove from burner and add the moonshine. Working in batches, puree soup in blender and return to pot. Add the cream a little at a time and sprinkle with nutmeg and salt. When serving add a sprig of rosemary or tyme.

Granny said a good bowl of soup and cornbread is about all you really needed to keep your motor operating in fine fashion. I believe she meant it's just enough to be satisfying and filling.

# Spiked Taco Soup

| | |
|---|---|
| 2 lbs. lean hamburger | 1-14oz. can corn drained |
| 1-14oz. can crushed tomatoes | 1 cup spring water |
| 1-14oz. kidney beans drained | 1 pkg. taco seasoning |
| 6 green onions chopped | 1 red bell pepper diced |
| 2-3 T. moonshine | nachos & grated cheese |

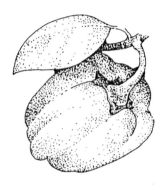

In a skillet brown the hamburger, onions and pepper.
Drain and place meat in a large heavy pot. Add all other
ingredients but the moonshine, nachos and cheese. Stir
until well blended turn heat to low and cook for about
one hour. Add the moonshine one tablespoon at a time.
Serve in bowl with grated cheese and nachos crumbled
on top. Ole, ya'll!

## Crocked Tomato Soup

| | |
|---|---|
| 1 small hot onion diced | 2 T. melted butter |
| 1 14 ½ oz.canned tomatoes diced | 1 ½ T. chopped basil |
| 1 ½ cups chicken broth | 1 tsp. tyme |
| 1 8oz. can tomato sauce | 2 T. moonshine |
| white pepper and salt to taste | extra basil |

In large saucepan cook the onion only until tender. Add the whole can of tomatoes, broth, herbs and pepper. Bring to a boil; reduce heat; add the moonshine turn burner to simmer and cover and simmer thirty minutes. Place soup in a blender or food processor bowl. Cover and blend on process until smooth. Pour back into the pan; heat through. Four servings. Garnish with basil.

I asked Granny what she and other ladies used in her day when there were no crock pots. She said she used a pot and the stove but couldn't speak for the other ladies!

# Chunky Cheesy Ham Bone Tater Soup

4 medium potatoes diced
1 ham bone
2 T. moonshine
1 cup heavy cream
1 cup shredded cheddar cheese

1 small onion diced
4 pats butter
3 cups sweet milk
salt to taste

Pour water to cover ham bone in a heavy pot and boil for about twenty minutes. Place your rinsed diced potatoes and onion in the cooking pot; if needed add enough water to cover the potatoes. Cook until very tender. Remove the ham bone and all but one cup of the liquid. With a potato masher, mash down in the pan a couple of times; add the butter, milk and cream. Simmer and remove from heat and add the moonshine. Will serve four or five city folks. Serve soup with sprinkled cheese.

Granny said she's never seen anyone turn down a bowl of her tater soup. No wonder. Between the moonshine and cheese who would say "no."

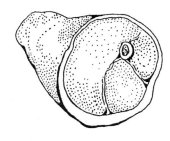

## Corn Chowder with Moonshine

| | |
|---|---|
| 4-5 ears of corn | 1 cup diced, peeled potato |
| ½ cup chopped onion | ½ cup spring water |
| 1 cup chicken stock | 2 cups sweet milk |
| 1 T. butter | 2 T. flour |
| 2 T. moonshine | salt to taste |

Garnishes (crumbled bacon or chives)

Cut the corn off the cob and place in heavy saucepan, this should be at least two cups; add the potato, water, onion and chicken stock. Bring to boil; cover, reduce heat to simmer until corn and potaoes are tender. Stir in 1 ½ cups milk and butter. Combine remaining milk and flour in a cup and blend. Stir into the corn mixture, continually stirring until thick. Remove from heat and add the moonshine. Serve immediately with garnish of bacon or chives.

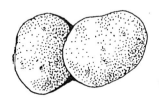

This soup gives you corn from the cob and corn from a little old brown jug.

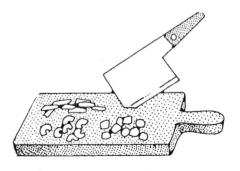

## Pea Soup Spiked

1 ½ cups dry split peas
3 smoked ham hocks
1 bay leaf
¾ cup chopped celery
1 T. butter
salt and pepper to taste

5 cups chicken broth
¼ tsp. marjoram crushed
¾ cup chopped carrots
¾ cup chopped onion
2 T. moonshine
chives

Rinse peas. In large pot combine peas, broth, meat, marjoram and bring to a boil. Reduce heat and simmer for one hour. Stir occasionally. Remove hocks and when cool cut the meat off and return to pot. Add the carrot, celery and onion. Add more broth if needed. Return to boil; reduce heat and simmer covered for thirty minutes. Add the butter and moonshine. Add the chives on top when ladled into bowls. You may substitute with diced smoked ham instead of hocks. Serves five hearty eaters.

Here in the mountains we don't go by bowls full. We would say it feeds two deer hunters and possibly one bass fisherman that didn't get his catch!

## Moonshine Minestrone

2 ½ cups spring water          ½ cup chopped carrots
¼ cup chopped celery           ½ chopped onion
2 tsp. beef bouillon granules  1 clove garlic minced
½ tsp. dried oregano           ½ tsp. dried basil
½ tsp. pepper                  ½ cup chopped cabbage
½ chopped zucchini             2 T. tiny macaroni
4 bacon strips fried           2-3 T. moonshine
1 15oz. can drained white northern beans
1-7 ½ oz. can tomatoes diced

In large pot put the water, carrot, onion, celery, bouillon, garlic, basil and oregano. Bring to a boil and add macaroni and tomatoes; reduce heat. Cover, simmer fifteen minutes. Stir in beans, cabbage, and zucchini. Return to a boil; reduce heat, cover and simmer for ten minutes. Add the moonshine 1 tablespoon at a time. Crumble bacon on top.

Soup fixin' and winter snow goes together like grits and eggs. Add the fire of moonshine and it will heat every part of your body. Granny says that at her and Pappy's age they need a little extra fire for medicinal purposes.

# Main Dishes

Here in the south as parts elsewhere, we have something in common. We love to cook, eat and feed. Asking for second helpings will have the cooks beaming with pride. We page through hundreds of recipes and glue ourselves in front of our televisions with pen and paper ready to copy another recipe from a chef or heading out to purchase cookbooks, continually seeking ways to make our taste buds jump for joy and our palates sigh with sheer contentment. Our bellies are not satisfied with the same old same old anymore. They have united and gone on strike. Their demands are simple and negotiable. They desire taste and flavor. Night after night we hear, what's for supper? Wouldn't you love to respond at least once, moonshine!

In the past we could hardly wait to be called to supper and someone at the table would remark how good the food tasted and inquire what the amazing flavor that tantalized their taste buds was. One of the ingredients used back then and possibly still in use today is found in that little brown jug hidden somewhere in the barn and is none other but good ole' moonshine. Once called "Granny's secret recipe" and only brought out for special occasions. We now boldly cook with every wine, beer and liquor to be found. As a true born and bred southerner I feel moonshine has never received the honor and attention that it deserves. I do ask when trying these recipes please cook responsibly and have a designated tee-totaler available to escort you from the kitchen to the dining room. And, if you continue to show signs of teetering when being set upright, please be gracious and excuse yourself while sliding from your chair down onto the floor with your apron now up around your armpits as you begin crawling hand over hand toward the door that you hope is leading to your bedroom with dignity like a true southern belle.

Be advised that no children are allowed to eat, drink or smell any recipe from this book and amateur cooks should not attempt to duplicate or manufacture these recipes without supervision of an experienced granny, who knows her way around the kitchen and moonshine. Moonshine is powerful and if'n you aint careful and use to much you may not have a mind. Stick with just the amounts called for in your recipes. Ya'll want the food to taste good; you aint out to kill it or yourselves!

# INDEX

## Creole Mountain Moonshine Way

| | |
|---|---|
| 30 medium shrimp | 3 ribs of celery |
| ½ cup chopped onion | 2 garlic cloves minced |
| ½ cup chopped bell pepper | 2 T. butter |
| 1-16oz. diced can tomatoes | 2 T. parsley snipped |
| salt to taste | ½ tsp. paprika |
| 1/8 tsp. ground red pepper | 1 bay leaf |
| 3 T. spring water | 4 tsp. cornstarch |
| 3 T. moonshine | 2 tsp. olive oil |
| 4 basil leaves snipped | ½ tsp. cane sugar |

In a large skillet melt the butter with the olive oil and cook onion, pepper, celery and garlic until tender. Add the tomatoes turn down the heat to simmer; add bay leaf, paprika, ground red pepper and salt and sugar, cover and simmer about 30 minutes. In a deep bowl put the shelled, and cleaned shrimp; add the the water and moonshine. Turn the shrimp every few minutes; add to the sauce and cook on medium until shrimp are tender. If you want the mixture thickened, mix cornstarch with two tablespoons water and add a little at a time. Remove bay leaf. Good with rice.

Uncle Claude likes this dish. And he's hard to please.

# Salmon in White Lighting

| | |
|---|---|
| 2 salmon steaks | 1 T. lemon juice |
| 2 T. olive oil | 1 tsp. rosemary crushed |
| 2 cloves garlic, minced | 1 tsp. fresh ground pepper |
| 2 T. moonshine | 3 T. spring water |
| 1 T. Worcestershire sauce | |

In a shallow pan add all the ingredients except the salmon. Rinse and blot salmon with paper towel; lay the salmon in the marinade to coat both sides. Cover and place in icebox for two hours, turn the salmon every little bit. Have the heat of your outdoor grill on medium. Oil the grill before placing the salmon. About four inches from the heat. Grill five minutes on each side or when flaky. Enjoy!

Ya'll remember now that moonshine and fire can be a little tricky. So stay with the grilling. You wouldn't want to catch something ablaze because of two little old fish! Watch out now!

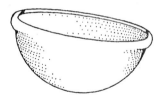

## Fried Gulf Red Snapper

| | |
|---|---|
| 6 fillet Red Snapper steaks | 2 T. flour |
| 1 ½ cups stone ground cornmeal | 1 tsp. salt |
| 1 tsp. pepper | 3 T. moonshine |
| 1 ½ cups real mayonnaise | 2 sliced lemons |
| 2 T. sweet drained relish | 1 shake hot sauce |
| ½ cup omega oil or olive oil | 1 tsp. dill |

In a bowl mix the mayonnaise, relish, hot sauce, dill, moonshine and juice from three slices of lemon. Cover and chill in icebox. Rinse the snapper and paper towel dry and lay on wax paper. In a shallow bowl put the flour, cornmeal, salt and pepper. In a deep iron skillet put the oil and set on a burner about medium high to get started and then turn to medium. Lay fish in and fry until flaky and brown. You may need a bit more oil. Drain on paper towels and serve with lemon wedges and tarter sauce.

I never knew that typing would give you the hungrys!

# Southern Soft Shell Crabs and Shrimp Stewed

| | |
|---|---|
| 8 fresh soft shell crabs | 32 fresh shrimp |
| 3 sliced lemons | 1 bay leaf |
| 1tsp. cayenne pepper | 2 garlic cloves |
| 1 T. salt | 1 T. peppercorns |
| very large pot | ¼ cup moonshine |

Fill water up half way in large stewing pot; add 1 whole lemon that is sliced, bay leaf, garlic, peppercorns, cayenne, salt and moonshine. Bring water to boil Put the live crabs (or frozen crabs) and the shrimp with the shells still on into pot and boil until the shrimp are pink. This can boil over so keep an eye on it. Turn the burner off and let the seafood sit in the water for ten minutes longer. Serve with lemon wedges. Good groceries.

Nothing makes a fisherman happier than sitting around a picnic table eating soft shell crabs and shrimp and telling fishing tales of how they almost caught the biggest Bass, Snapper and the biggest ocean Grouper that usually got away.

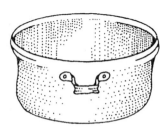

## Pork Loin and Slippery Moonshine Sauce

| | |
|---|---|
| 2 thin pork loins | 2 cups barbecue sauce |
| 3 T. olive oil | ½ cup chopped hot onion |
| 2 T. brown sugar | 2-3 T. moonshine |
| 1 tsp. garlic salt | 1 tsp. black pepper |
| crock pot | sandwich buns |

Rub the pork loins with the garlic salt and pepper. Set on wax paper. In heavy iron skillets put the olive oil and when the heat is about medium; put the loins in and brown on each side. Remove skillet from burner and lay the pork loins in crock pot; add the sauce, onion, brown sugar and moonshine over the loins. Cook on low for about six to eight hours. When cooked, remove the loins and shred the meat and return the meat to crock pot until you're ready to make the barbecue sandwiches. Good also with cold slaw.

Nothing is finer than smelling barbecue cooking in the kitchen and nothing is better tasting than getting your fair share of it. Your mouth will start watering long before it's done! Have patience. Feeds six city folks.

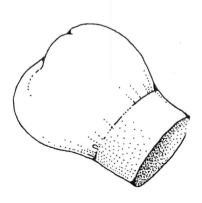

## Stir Fry Lighting Beef Tenderloin

1 medium beef tenderloin steak
1 cup broccoli florets
1 hot onion thinly wedged
½ cup sliced red bell pepper
2-3 T. olive oil
1 pkg. beef stir fry sauce
½ cup extra water

1 cup chopped celery
½ cup sliced almonds
½ cup cherry tomatoes
1 cup mushrooms
2 T. moonshine
2 tsp. black pepper

Partially freeze the beef so it will slice thinly. Sprinkle a little pepper on it. In wok heat 2 to 3T. oil and stir fry beef; remove and keep warm while you stir fry the remaining vegetables. Mix the package sauce with their directions. Return beef to wok and pour package ingredient mix in. Heat through and mix the moonshine and most of the water in a cup and pour also into the stir fry; heat. Good with rice or Chinese noodles. Serves 6.

If there's a cold mountain wind stirring and the men have been out chopping firewood all day, you'll be fortunate to get three servings.

## Mountain Stroganoff Soused

| | |
|---|---|
| 1 lb. lean ground beef | 1 clove garlic minced |
| ½ cup chopped onion | 2 T. moonshine |
| 2 cups beef bouillon | 3 T. sour cream |
| ¼ cups Italian bread crumbs | 1 egg |
| 2 T. chopped parsley | 3 T. olive oil |
| 1 T. sweet milk | ½ cup flour |
| 1 cup sliced fresh mushrooms | salt to taste |

In bowl mix the egg then bread crumbs and 1 T. parsley.
Add the beef and mix by hand and form small meatballs.
In a skillet add enough of the olive oil to coat the bottom
of pan. Roll the meatballs in flour and lay on wax paper.
Turn burner on medium under skillet and add meatballs
and brown on all sides. Remove meatballs to warming
plate. Drain most of the oil and then add the onions,
garlic and mushrooms and stir until tender. Add the
bouillon and moonshine; put the meatballs back in.
Simmer covered about twenty minutes. Mix 2 T. of
flour with added bouillon. Stir into stroganoff; add the
sour cream. Sounds like a good supper to me.

# Beef Stew and Moonshine

| | |
|---|---|
| 2 lbs. stew beef | 1 cup flour |
| 1 large hot onion | 4 chopped carrots |
| 2 ribs of celery chopped | 1 bay leaf |
| 1 can beef bouillon | 3 T. olive oil |
| 1 cup frozen peas thawed | 3 T. moonshine |
| 1 pkg. dry beef stew mix | 5 red potatoes |
| crock pot | |

Flour stew meat and fry on both sides until brown in heavy skillet with 3T. oil. Peel the potatoes and cut in quarters. Put the stew meat and all the vegetables except the peas in a heavy pot or crock pot. Mix the dry mix by directions and pour on the stew. Add the canned beef broth and moonshine and the bay leaf. Cook medium low on stove until meat is tender or in a crock pot for 8-10 hours on low. Last couple of minutes add the peas.

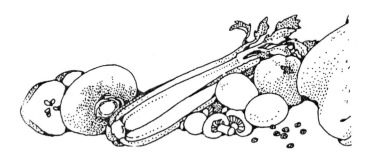

Aunt Guzzy says that this meal would satisfy even a king. Granny asked her if'n that included revenuers? Then they went on a laughing binge. They're a caution!

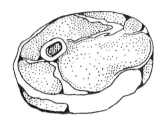

## Granny's Crocked Pot Roast

| | |
|---|---|
| 1 rump roast | 2 T. garlic powder |
| 2 T. onion powder | 2 T. black pepper |
| 1 tsp. salt | 1 pkg. onion soup mix |
| 1 cup fresh sliced mushrooms | 1 hot onion sliced |
| 1 beef bouillon cube | 2 T. oil |
| 3 T. moonshine | 1 tsp. cumin |

In dutch oven or cast iron pot, put the oil. Rinse and pat dry the roast and rub in the cumin, garlic and onion powder then the pepper and salt. Brown and sear beef in oil on all sides. Lay a few pieces of the onion in bottom of the crock pot and put the roast on top. Dilute the onion soup mix in 1 ½ cups of water and add the moonshine to it. Put the mushrooms around the roast. Pour the liquid over the roast and finish laying onion slices on and around the roast. Drop the bouillon cube in. Cook on low for 8 to 10 hours. Remove meat and thicken juices for gravy.

Pappy says Granny can outbake, outboil, outfry any moonshine cook in all the mountains and valleys. I think he's buttering her up for a sample of her fine cooking.

## Moonshine Chicken with Pasta

| | |
|---|---|
| 2 chicken breasts | ½ cup flour |
| 2 cans chicken broth | linguine pasta |
| ½ stick butter | 1 cup parsley chopped |
| 1 bunch spring onions chopped | 2 T. moonshine |
| ½ tsp rosemary crushed | 1 T. olive oil |
| 1 tsp. paprika | salt and pepper |

Wash the vegetables before cutting. Rinse, dry and flatten the chicken; dredge in flour, paprika, salt and pepper; lay on wax paper. In a deep frying pan melt the butter with the oil and stir fry the onion and mushrooms until tender; remove and keep warm; in the same pan add chicken and brown on both sides; add ¾ can of broth, ½ cup parsley and moonshine; simmer while preparing pasta. Remaining broth goes into a pasta pot; add enough water that will cook pasta; when tender then drain; add remaining parsley and serve.

The men folk may not be accustomed to eating this dish, and if they quiz you on what's in it; just cut the chase and say moonshine. They'll swallow it whole!

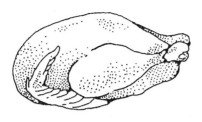

## Moonshine Chow Mien

| | |
|---|---|
| 2 cups cooked chicken chopped | 2 ribs celery chopped |
| 1 sm. onion chopped | 2 cans chicken broth |
| 1 cup bean sprouts (fresh) | 3 T. moonshine |
| 4 tsp. cornstarch | 2 T. spring water |
| ½ cup diced red bell pepper | salt to taste |

Put all ingredients except cornstarch and water in big stewing pot. Simmer until vegetables are tender; mix water and cornstarch; add a little at a time until the thickness you want. Serve over rice or noodles.

Cooks, this quick easy meal is good for the days when you're late getting home from a meeting of the Ladies Ridge Runner Garden Club. Granny would say you were having an attack of the lazys!

# Chicken Cacciatore with a Kick

2 ½ lbs of chicken thighs
3 cloves garlic
1 cup mushrooms sliced
1 pint chopped tomatoes
1 cup chicken broth
1 bay leaf
½ tsp. oregano
fresh grated Parmesan

½ cup chopped onion
1-2 T. olive oil
1- 8oz. can tomato sauce
¼ cup moonshine
2 T. basil snipped
4 tsp. cornstarch
fettuccine pasta
2 T. spring water

Skin chicken, rinse and pat dry. In a large skillet fry the chicken, onion and garlic in the oil until lightly brown. Put all the other ingredients in except the cornstarch and pasta. Bring to boil, reduce heat and simmer about 35 minutes or when the chicken is fully cooked. Throw away bay leaf. Mix cornstarch and 2 T. water and pour into mixture and stir briskly. Cook pasta, dip the sauce on and lay chicken on the side; grate cheese on top of pasta. Serves 4.

Cousin Bubba would say this here is good vittles!

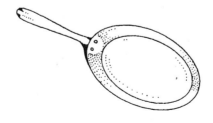

## Country Cured Ham with Shine

2 large slices cured salty ham          1 T. molasses
2 cups strong brewed coffee             1 T. moonshine
ground black pepper                         shortening

In a large cast iron skillet melt enough shortening to cover the bottom of the pan. Cut the ham into small slices and pepper both sides generously. You may need to add more shortening. Turn heat to medium and lay the ham slices in and brown both sides. Drain on paper towels. Cover ¾ of the ham in foil to keep warm. Drain most of the shortening from skillet, remove from heat and add the remaining ¼ ham slices, molasses and coffee; cook until hot. Remove from burner; add the moonshine. Pour gravy into a bowl. This is a hungry man's breakfast along side the grits, fried eggs, fresh churned butter, buttermilk biscuits and molasses.

Pappy would sure enough give Granny a peck on the cheek for this breakfast. Shoot, so would I!

Ham Glazed Over

| | |
|---|---|
| 1 spiral sugar cured ham | 3 T. moonshine |
| 1 T. mustard | 3 T. clover honey |
| ½ tsp. ground cloves | |

Bake the ham per instructions wrapped in foil. Mix moonshine, mustard, cloves and honey. When ham is baked remove from oven; open the foil and spread over the hot ham; reseal the foil around the ham and let it set for about 30 minutes before serving the spiral slices.

This will feed a holiday party crowd in fine fashion. With the shine in the ham, ya'll want need to serve drinks, maybe a little spring water to wash it down! Remember now, alcohol food is just for adults.

## MOONSHINE DESSERTS

Since some of ya'll are not familiar with weights and measures that we southerners use, I thought I would explain some of them to you.

Hand full = one cup
Smidgen = ½ teaspoon
Touch = one short quick shake
Thimble full = almost a teaspoon
Tad = 1/8 of a cup or less
Pinch= 1 teaspoon
Sprinkle = dusting
Big canning jar full = 1 quart
Small canning jar full = pint
Jelly glass = almost a ½ pint

Now some of these measurements may be a bit off, but most cooks never divulge the entire amount that's needed to duplicate their prize recipes. Granny always wins the coveted moonshine cook off here in the mountains and she plans to keep the recipe to herself. Let me give you a scenario.

Granny's favorite sister, Aunt Dorcas, and Granny
are always competing in the mountain moonshine cook
off and Aunt Dorcas asked Granny for her prize winning
moonshine pot roast recipe. Granny smiled and said,
"Why sugar, it's a little of this, and a little bit of that,
and not near as much of either, but a whole lot of the
other." What she said was, no way sugar!

# Pies, Cobblers & Custards

# INDEX

## Granny's Peachy Lighting Cobbler

6-7 cups fresh sliced peaches
1 stick butter
1 cup cane sugar
1 egg beaten
1 T. moonshine

½ tsp. cinnamon
1 cup flour
1 tsp. baking powder
3 T. sweet milk

Put peaches and moonshine in an 8x8x2-inch baking dish with ¾ cup sugar, 1 T. flour, cinnamon and fold. Put pats of butter on top about a half stick. In a bowl mix flour and baking powder; cut the remaining butter in until coarse. Mix egg and milk. Add to the flour mixture just to moisten. Drop mixture into 6 mounds atop peaches and spread over the top gently. Bake at 375 oven about 25 minutes or when a toothpick inserted comes out clean. Serve with vanilla or peach ice cream.

Serves 6 city folks or 3 mountain men who are full up on supper.

## Blackberry Bottom Twang

6-7 cups fresh blackberries  1 ½ cups cane sugar
1 stick butter  2 T. flour
1 tsp. moonshine  1 tsp. lemon juice
2 T. sweet milk  1 pie crust

Mix berries, sugar flour, lemon juice and moonshine in an 8x8x2- baking dish. Melt butter and fold in your mixture. A prepared rolled pie crust (find in dairy case), wet the edging of pan with water; lay crust on and crimp to edging. Make air holes so steam can escape. With pastry brush dipped into milk spread on the crust. Sprinkle lightly with sugar. Bake 375 oven until golden brown. Also good with cold vanilla ice cream oozing down on the hot cobbler.

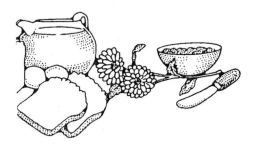

Ya'll will know who ate the most because they will have a purple mouth. At my house, it's all of us.

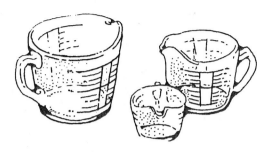

## Mountain Cherry Pie

| | |
|---|---|
| 6 cups tart pitted cherries | 1 ¼ cups cane sugar |
| 1 tsp. lemon juice | 1 tsp. moonshine |
| 2 T. cornstarch | 2 T. butter |
| dash of cinnamon | 2- 9" crusts |
| 2 drops red food coloring | 2 T. sweet milk |
| ½ tsp. almond extract | |

In a bowl put the cherries, food color, almond extract, moonshine and lemon juice; add the sugar and cornstarch and fold. Spoon the cherry mixture into a 9" crust; dot with butter. Lay the top crust on and cut to fit around the edge but do not crimp (as it bakes, it will seal). With a pastry brush dipped in milk, brush the top of the crust. Place the pie in the middle of a foiled lined cookie sheet and make air holes in top crust for steam; bake 375 for one hour or until nice and brown.

This pie recipe could win bragging rights!

# Apple Pie with Moonshine

| | |
|---|---|
| ¾ cups cane sugar | 3 T. flour |
| ½ tsp cinnamon | ½ tsp allspice |
| 1 tsp. moonshine | butter |
| 2 - 9" pie crusts | 1 tsp. lemon juice |
| 2 T. sweet milk | |

6 cups tart apples pared & sliced thin

Put apples, spices, sugar, moonshine, lemon juice and flour in a bowl and fold the fruit. Spoon apples into pie crust and dot with butter; lay top crust on and cut to fit pan but do not crimp the edges (it will seal itself); make air holes for steam to escape. On a foiled lined cookie sheet pan set pie in center of foil. With a pastry brush dipped in milk brush top of pie; bake at 375 for one hour to 1 ½ hours until brown.

Pappy and his cousin, Wilbur, once entered a pie eating contest and both men tied for first place; Granny said the men swore off apple eating for an entire fall season.

# Apple Slippery Dumplings

6 tart peeled, quartered apples
1 ½ cups brown sugar
1 stick butter
1 tsp. vanilla extract
1 T. moonshine

1 can flaky biscuits
1 cup chopped pecans
1 ¼ cup spring water
1 tsp. cinnamon

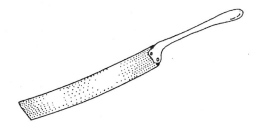

Unroll the biscuits. From the 10 can biscuits flake apart to make 20 biscuits total. Take 2 quarters of each apple and press dough around and set each into an 8x8x2-baking dish. Lay remaining dough on top. You should have 12 dumplings when completed. In a bowl put the brown sugar, cinnamon and nuts and blend with a fork; set aside. In a heavy sauce pot put the water, moonshine butter and vanilla. Bring to a boil making sure butter has melted; pour over the apple dumplings; sprinkle the sugar mixture on top of the dumplings. Bake in oven at 350 for one hour. Crust is beautiful!

Your guests will want more so why not just whip up 2 pans while you're at it. Enjoy ya'll!

# Moonshine Raisin Pie

½ cup brown sugar
2 cups raisins
½ cup orange juice
1 tsp. moonshine
2- 9" pie crusts
2 T. sweet milk

2 T. cornstarch
1 ½ tsp orange zest
1 ½ T. lemon juice
½ cup chopped pecans
1 1/3 cups spring water
2 T. butter

In a saucepan mix the brown sugar, cornstarch; add the raisins, zest, lemon and orange juice, butter, water and moonshine; cook just to boiling point. Remove from heat; stir in the nuts. Spoon into pie crust; lay second crust on top and cut to fit edging of pan, but don't seal; it seals itself. Cut slits in top crust for steam to escape. Dip pastry brush in the milk and spread on the top of pie. Cover edge with foil. Bake on a cookie sheet lined with foil at 375 for 25 minutes and then remove the foil from the edge and bake another 20 minutes. Crust will be nice and flaky. Feeds 8 city folks.

Aunt Sadie says she always saves her dried up raisins for this pie. Uncle Claude says if'n Sadie would spend as much time in the kitchen as she does listening in on the party line the raisins wouldn't have a chance to dry up!

## Snookered Strawberry Rhubarb Crisp

| | |
|---|---|
| 3 cups thinly cut rhubarb | 1 cup cane sugar |
| 3 cups fresh halved strawberries | 1 ¼ cups brown sugar |
| ½ cup rolled oats | ¼ cup flour |
| ½ tsp.ginger | ¼ cup butter |
| ¼ cup pecans | 1 T. moonshine |
| 1 tsp. vanilla extract | 1 tsp. lemon juice |

In bowl put the rhubarb, strawberries and lemon juice; add the moonshine, 1 cup cane sugar, ¼ cup brown sugar and 2 T. flour and vanilla extract. Fold. For topping, in a mixing bowl combine, oats, brown sugar, remaining flour, ginger; cut in butter until crumbly; stir in nuts. Sprinkle over the top of fruit. Bake 375 for 30-35 minutes until it turns a golden brown. Vanilla ice cream would go nicely with this. Serves 6 city folks.

Granny calls this plain old comfort food. Pappy calls it just plain old good!

# Pineapple Grated Cheese Squares

2- 8oz. blocks cream cheese      1 cup cane sugar
2 large cans crushed pineapple  1 T. moonshine
2 sm. boxes instant                  2 cups sweet milk
   cheesecake pudding mixes      2 tsp. cornstarch
1 cup finely shredded sharp cheese

Drain both cans of pineapple thoroughly into a
saucepan; add ¾ cup sugar, moonshine and cornstarch.
Cook until slightly thickened; set aside until room
temperature.  In deep mixing bowl beat the softened
cream cheese with ¼ cup sugar; add the pudding mixes
and milk.  Beat for a minute or two. (This is thick).  Add
the sharp cheese and pineapple. Mix with wooden spoon
and spread into a long dish.  Pour pineapple sauce
completely over the mixture.  Cover and put in the
icebox at leat 4 hours.  Serve in cut squares.

This dessert could be the talk of the Mountain Valley
Ladies Auxiliary or, the front porch tea gathering.
Gussy this dessert up by serving it on your good china.

## Blueberry Cheese Cake

2- 8oz. cream cheese
1 cup sweet milk
1 sm. box instant
   cheesecake pudding mix
1 T. moonshine
1 T. cornstarch

3 cups fresh blueberries
1-9" graham cracker crust
¾ cups cane sugar
1 tsp. vanilla extract
½ cup spring water
1 tsp. lemon juice

In a saucepan put the water, lemon juice, moonshine and 2 cups blueberries cook until starting to bubble good; add the ½ cup sugar mixed with 1 T. cornstarch which has been mixed with 1T. water. When bubbly but not to thick remove from heat and set aside until room temperature. In deep mixing bowl beat the softened cream cheeese untill fluffy; add the milk and pudding mix (mixture is thick) and fold in the 1 cup remaining blueberries. Pour blueberry filling on top and store in icebox at least 4-6 hours. Serves 8 city folks.

The reason I say use spring water; it's pure. I tasted city water once. Can't say I liked it much.

## Pecan Pie Mixed with Shine

3 jumbo brown eggs
1/3 cup cane sugar
1/3 cup butter melted
1 ¼ cups pecans halved
1-9" pie crust

1 cup corn syrup
1/3 cup brown sugar
1 tsp. vanilla extract
1 tsp. moonshine
dash of salt

In mixing bowl put the eggs and mix on low; add and stir with a spoon the syrup, both sugars, moonshine, butter, salt and vanilla extract. Stir real good. Add the nuts and stir a couple of times. Pour gently into the pie crust. Cover edge with foil. On a foil lined cookie sheet place the pie in the center and bake in a 350 oven for 25 minutes; remove foil; bake 20 minutes longer. Makes 8 very tasty slices.

Ladies, if ya'll are real bakers you don't need perfume; you always smell like baked goods and the men folk prefer that anyway. Dab a little vanilla behind your ears and try it out!

## Lemon or Lime Pie on a Toot

2 lime custard yogurts     1 lime gelatin
¼ cup cane sugar     2 limes sliced thin & drained
1-8oz. cream cheese     1 tsp. moonshine
1-8oz. whip topping     1-9" graham cracker crust
¼ cup boiling water

In medium mixing bowl beat softened cream cheese until smooth; fold in cool whip; set aside. In medium bowl put the gelatin, sugar, moonshine and water. Stir vigorously; fold in the lime yogurts; fold in the cream cheese mixture (there will be pieces of lime gelatin) and spoon into crust. Lay a few slices of lime on the top and store in icebox 6 hours prior to serving. Put a lime slice on each piece when serving. Do the same way for lemon pie. You should get 8 nice slices.

Cousin Blanche would say it was 'passable'. Granny said if'n Cousin Blanche had been the one coming up with the recipe she would swear the pie deserved a blue ribbon!

## Deep Chocolate Moonshine Pie

4 extra large egg yolks    1 ½ tsp. vanilla
½ cup sugar    ¼ cup cornstarch
1 tsp. moonshine    1 T. butter
8 oz. carton chocolate topping    1 cup heavy cream
½ cup chocolate sprinkles    1- 9" baked pie crust
2 oz. unsweetened chocolate    2 cups sweet milk

In medium saucepan combine sugar and cornstarch; gradually stir in milk and heavy cream and unsweetened chocolate. Cook and stir over medium-high heat until thick. In a bowl beat egg yolks lightly with a fork. Gradually stir in 1 cup of the hot filling into yolks. Pour into the pudding and cook 2 more minutes more. Remove from heat; stir in butter, moonshine and vanilla; pour into pastry shell. Cool on a wire rack. When room temperature, store in icebox. When completely chilled; add chocolate topping on and then chocolate sprinkles. Good! Good! Good!

# Double Tasty Cheesecake

2-8oz. blocks cream cheese
½ cup coconut
1 cup maraschino cherries
1 cup mandarin oranges
1 sm. box instant vanilla

1 cup sweet milk
½ chopped pecans
1 cup crushed pineapple
1-2 T. moonshine
1-9" graham cracker crust

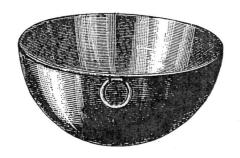

Drain cherries and set on a paper towels and wax paper. Drain the pineapple and the oranges and pour the moonshine in the pineapple. In a deep mixing bowl beat the softened cream cheese until fluffy; add the pudding and milk and beat on medium just until blended; fold in the fruits and nuts and then spread into the crust. Cover with wax paper and chill in icebox 6 hours. Serves 8 city folks.

Ya'll, I think this is one classy dessert, the fruit mixed with the shine makes the fruit tipsy and it's a keeper! Enjoy it. I'm sure the ladies here in the holler will.

# MOONSHINE CAKES

There is one sure thing about bakers. Least wise with us mountain women. When we're baking, we're thinking and can't be bothered. Baking cakes takes patience and our families know they had best find some outdoor activity like chores to keep them busy so the cakes want fall looking like fritters. Then when they have baked to perfection, we wave our aprons out the backdoor for the all clear signal. We take our cake baking serious and when the Mountain Holler Bake Off approaches in the fall we start those creative juices flowing. Its sister against sister; mother against daughter-inlaw. We tell no one what delicious creation we're working on. It's an all out baking war. We love it!

Granny usually wins and gets the coveted first prize of a calico bibbed apron. Granny's cakes have always had a special delectable something or other that the judges preferred. The other ladies were puzzled by this until we found out through the gossip vine that Pappy told Elmer, who told Maudie who then got on the party line about Granny's moonshine baking secret. One of us ladies might be doing the winning cake walk strut yet wearing the new calico ruffled apron. We'll all use moonshine.

Needless to say when Granny found out that it was Pappy who divulged her secret we became sort of concerned for the old gent. Granny made him sleep in the barn for a week. Pappy didn't care. That's where the little old brown jug was being kept and that was all the company he needed.

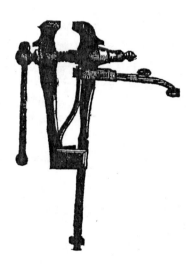

# Cakes

# INDEX

## Mountain Pound Cake

| | |
|---|---|
| 2 sticks butter softened | ½ cup shortening |
| 3 cups sifted flour | 3 cups cane sugar |
| ½ cup cream | 8 oz. sour cream |
| ½ tsp. salt | 1 tsp baking powder |
| ½ tsp. baking powder | 5 extra large brown eggs |
| 1 tsp. lemon flavoring | 1 tsp. vanilla extract |
| 1 tsp. almond flavoring | 2 T. moonshine |

Cream butter, shortening and sugar; add eggs one at a time blend; add baking powder, salt, sour cream, flour, cream, moonshine and flavorings. Mix well. Bake in a 325 oven on bottom rack for 1 ½ hours.

The south wouldn't be the south without a pound cake or two in our freezers. Good with fruit or custards.

## Pumpkin Cake with Shine Glaze

2 ½ cups flour
1 tsp. baking powder
1 tsp cinnamon
½ tsp. salt
¾ cups canned pumpkin
2 extra large brown eggs
1 ½ cups powdered sugar

1 cup brown sugar
½ cup pure cane sugar
2 T. orange juice
¾ cup buttermilk
¼ cup mountain honey
2 T. moonshine

In a bowl combine flour, white and brown sugars, baking powder and cinnamon. Add buttermilk, shortening, pumpkin and honey. Beat with electric mixer on medium for about a minute; add eggs and beat 2 minutes. Pour into a greased 13x9x2-inch baking pan. Bake on 350 for about 30-35 minutes. Mix the powdered sugar, orange juice and moonshine and pour over the warm cake. Poke holes in cake so it can seep in.

People pick at this cake and say they don't want a whole piece and continue to nibble at it until they picked the cake plate clean.

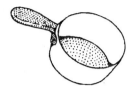

## Drunken Chocolate Torte

2 ½ cups powdered sugar
1 cup semisweet chocolate pieces
1 cup chopped pecans
½ cup sour dairy cream

½ cup brown sugar
2 T. moonshine
1 chocolate cake mix
1 stick butter

In microwave melt ½ stick of butter. Grease 2- 9" cake pans. Pour the butter equally in bottom of pans; sprinkle brown sugar on top and then the pecans; set aside. Mix chocolate cake mix as directed and add 1 T. moonshine beat 1 more minute. Pour mixture evenly in cake pans. Bake at 325 for 35 minutes or till a toothpick comes out clean (ovens vary). Remove from oven and let set a minute and flip the cakes gently from pans (the pecan glaze will be the top) unto butter greased foil sheets. Cool before frosting. For frosting melt ½ stick butter and chocolate pieces in a saucepan and remove from heat and stir in 1 T. moonshine; cool for 6 minutes and stir in sour cream and pour into mixing bowl with the powdered sugar, beating till smooth. Chocolate and moonshine, Pappy's dream come true and also for a few other folks.

## Sour Cream Soused Coffee Cake

| | |
|---|---|
| 1 ¼ cup cake flour | ¾ cup brown sugar |
| ¼ tsp. salt | 1/3 cup butter |
| 1 tsp baking powder | ¼ tsp. baking soda |
| ½ tsp. cinnamon | ¼ tsp. nutmeg |
| ½ cup dairy sour cream | 1 beaten jumbo egg |
| ¼ cup chopped pecans | 2 T. moonshine |

Combine flour, brown sugar and salt; cut in butter till crumbly; set aside ¼ cup crumb mixture. To remaining mixture add baking powder, baking soda, spices and mix well. Add sour cream, moonshine and egg and mix. Spread batter into a greased 8x8x2-inch baking pan. Stir reserved crumbs and sprinkle on top of batter. Bake at 350 for 30 minutes or till a toothpick inserted near center comes out clean.

Serve this with spring tea for the Ladies Auxilliary. They will be high stepping it by the time the meeting adjourns. Granny says they'll fly higher than a kite!

## Pineapple Upside Down Valley Cake

| | |
|---|---|
| 1 pineapple cake mix | 4 T. butter melted |
| 2/3 cup brown sugar | 10 maraschino cherries |
| 1 large can sliced pineapple | 3 T. moonshine |
| 3 T. cane sugar | |

Pour melted butter in a greased (with butter) 13x9x2-inch baking pan. Stir in sugar and 2 T. water. Half the drained cherries and pour the pineapple juice in small sauce pan; add the cane sugar and moonshine. Heat until sugar has dissolved and add one pat of butter. Remove from heat. Arrange pineapple slices and cherries in the pan. You should have a few remaining. Prepare cake mix by directions and spoon over the fruit into the pan. Bake in 350 oven for 30 to 35 minutes. Check doneness with a toothpick. Remove. Loosen the sides and flip on to a buttered cookie sheet. Make a few holes in cake with a fork and pour the moonshine mixture evenly on top. Use remaining fruit as decoration on the serving dishes.

Easy to make and no one will believe it started with a mix. Granny said it's none of their bees wax (business).

## Hot Fudge Sundae Cake

1 cup flour
¾ cup cane sugar
2 T. cocoa
2 tsp. baking powder
¼ tsp. salt
1 ¾ cup hot spring water
2 T. moonshine

1 tsp. vanilla extract
1 cup nuts chopped
1 cup brown sugar
¼ cup cocoa
½ cup sweet milk
2 T. Salad oil

In ungreased 9x9x2 pan stir flour, cane sugar, 2T. cocoa, baking powder and salt. Mix in milk, oil, and vanilla with a fork; stir in nuts; sprinkle with brown sugar and ¼ cup cocoa. Put the moonshine in the water and pour over batter. Bake 40 minutes in a 350 oven. Serve warm. Remember moonshine is in the oven. Watch it!

Mountain men like this hot cake with chocolate ice cream on it and chocolate syrup oozing on top. Our men folk do enjoy their sweets as well as the contents of the little brown jug.

## Applesauce and Moonshine Cake

2 cups flour
1 tsp. baking powder
1 ¼ tsp. cinnamon
¼ cup buttermilk
¼ cup butter softened
1 tsp. vanilla extract
1 T. moonshine

1 ½ cups cane sugar
1 tsp. soda
1 tsp. nutmeg
1 cup applesauce
¼ cup shortening
3 large brown eggs

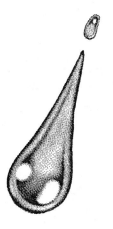

In a bowl combine flour, sugar, baking powder, soda and spices. Add buttermilk, butter, shortening, moonshine and vanilla. Beat on low 2 minutes; add eggs and beat on medium 2 minutes more. Pour batter into greased 13x9x2-inch baking pan. Bake in 350 oven for 30 minutes. Check doneness with a toothpick. Serves 12 city folks or 6 strapping mountain loggers.

The wonderful aroma coming from this cake tends to make your mouth water up. YUMMY!

## Peanut Butter Topping Cake

chocolate cake mix
1½ tsp. vanilla extract
½ cup peanuts crushed
1 tsp. moonshine

1 box powdered sugar
½ cup peanut butter
¼ cup sweet milk

Bake 2- 9" round cakes per directions on the box.  In mixing bowl; put peanut butter, moonshine, 1 cup powdered sugar and vanilla.  Beat well.  Add milk and remainder of powdered sugar.  Beat until creamy.  Frost the cake and sprinkle with peanuts.  Delicious!

Granny laughed and told me a story that one time Aunt Dorcas served this very cake recipe to her club meeting and she overheard a lady say that she bet she could make this cake even better, so Aunt Dorcas got fired up and snatched the fork and plate from her and pointed the woman to the cook stove and said, make your own cake.

## Lemon Cake with Shine

3 cups pure cane sugar

1 cup shortening

1 stick butter softened

6 large brown eggs

4 cups cake flour

2 T. moonshine

1-6oz. can frozen lemonade thawed

½ tsp. baking powder

1 cup sweet milk

1tsp. vanilla extract

2 tsp. lemon extract

½ tsp salt

2 cups powdered sugar

Cream shortening, sugar and butter.  Add and beat in eggs one at a time.  Alternate with milk and dry ingredients; add flavorings. Grease and flour a tube pan; pour mixture in and bake in lower rack at 350 for 1 ½ hours.  Cool in pan 20 minutes. Prick warm cake with a cake tester through to the bottom.  Mix lemonade, powder sugar and moonshine; spoon over cake. Let set for at least 15 minutes and remove from pan.  Dust with powder sugar when cut into serving slices.

Good tasting doesn't hardly begin to describe this cake. This might be the very cake that will win the Mountain Holler Bake Off.

# Prune Cake Done Right

| | |
|---|---|
| 1 cup vegetable oil | 1 tsp. cinnamon |
| 1 ½ cups pure cane sugar | 1 tsp. nutmeg |
| 3 extra large brown eggs | 1 tsp. allspice |
| 2 cups flour | 1 cup buttermilk |
| ½ tsp. salt | 1 ¼ cup stewed prunes |
| 1 T. baking soda | 1 cup pecans chopped |
| ½ tsp. baking powder | 1 T. moonshine |

Cream oil, sugar and eggs. Mix dry ingredients alternating with buttermilk. Add moonshine, prunes and pecans. Pour into a well greased and floured deep tube pan and bake for 40 minutes or until toothpick inserted comes out clean. A wonderful breakfast cake.

Some folks shy away from prunes for one reason or another but I betcha your men folk wouldn't snub their noses up over eating prunes prepared this way.

## Gingerbread Spiced

1 ½ cups flour        ¼ cup brown sugar
¾ tsp. cinnamon       ¾ tsp. ginger
½ tsp baking powder    ½ tsp soda
½ cup shortening      ½ cup black strap molasses
1 T. moonshine        1 jumbo egg
½ cup spring water

In mixing bowl combine all dry ingredients. Add the
shortening, molasses, egg, moonshine and water. Beat
with electric mix on low until mixed and then on
medium for 2 minutes. Pour into greased and floured
8x8x2-inch baking pan. Bake at 350 for 35 minutes or
till toothpick inserted near the center comes out lean.

The recipe feeds 9 city folks or 4 of our mountain men.
It would have fed 5 mountain men but a few men got
wind that Granny had warm gingerbread in the house
and sent poor cousin Wilbur with his dog Bo, on a wild
goose chase looking for lost moonshine jugs.

# Banana Cake with Moonshine

2 cups flour        1 ½ cups cane sugar
1 ½ tsp. baking powder      ¾ tsp. baking soda
1 ½ cups mashed ripe bananas    ½ cup buttermilk
½ cup shortening      2 extra large brown eggs
1 tsp. vanilla extract      1 tsp. moonshine
½ cup chopped pecans      ½ tsp. salt
1- 8 oz. Container whip topping

Preheat oven to 350. Grease and flour a 13x9x2-inch baking pan and set aside. In bowl combine dry ingredients. Add bananas, buttermilk, shortening, eggs, moonshine and vanilla. Beat with mixer on low speed to combine. Beat on medium speed for 3 minutes. Pour into pan and bake 30 minutes or till a toothpick comes out clean. Cool completely and spread the topping over the cake and sprinkle the pecans over the topping. Store in icebox covered. Serves 12.

Granny got mad at Pappy for eating up all the ripened bananas she had saved for the cake and Pappy told her she should be thanking him because he did her a favor by eating up all the nanners, seeing how she almost let them go to the bad. Sparks flew on that day!

## Special Fruitcake

Ya'll this fruitcake recipe I'm sharing with you was giving to me from a mountain recipe that my Granny handed down to me. She had me copy it down while we were sitting on her front porch indulging ourselves on Moonshine Sippers and that should tell you something. Naturally the ingredient that makes it special is the moonshine. Once I mastered the baking of this fruitcake with Granny's guidance, she was delighted when she saw the results and she felt I should send it to her sister, Aunt Mae, who at that time said I was her favorite niece and the only one of her relatives with a lick of sense; sorry to say I proved her wrong. My aunt lived in the deep mountain holler valley and Granny said Aunt Mae would be honored to receive it since Mae thought I was so special and the only family member with a lick of sense, so we sent it to her.

Several days passed and I received a telephone call from Aunt Mae that she had gotten the fruitcake and it looked elegant so she felt it fitting to serve as the refreshment for the Women's Mission Temperance Society from her church that had their meeting at her house the night before, she also wanted me to know that she was the chairwoman. Aunt Mae said the ladies all got the giggles after eating the cake and one or two couldn't keep steady on their feet. When their husbands arrived to tote the good ladies home from the temperance meeting they swore their wives had been indulging in the wild fruit of the vine. Aunt Mae asked me where I got the recipe and what the ingredients were that went into the cake.

I told her Granny gave me her secret recipe and I started reciting the ingredients in the fruitcake and how Granny had me add a little more shine to make it extra special. Aunt Mae then asked exactly how much more shine and I told her a half of a jelly jar full. The other end of the line went dead. I think she fainted. Here's Granny's secret fruitcake recipe. You decipher for yourselves. Set oven to 350; grease and flour a big tube pan, spoon in mixture and bake until heavy as a brick.

1 hand full of chopped pecans
1 hand full chopped English walnuts
½ regular jelly glass of chopped black walnuts
½ regular jelly glass of chopped almonds
½ hand full for both raisins and snipped dates
1 hand full candied cherries chopped
1 good size hand full of dried citrus
½ hand full dried pineapple
½ hands full of brown sugar and pure cane sugar
2 extra large brown eggs
2 hands full flour
½ small jelly jar of orange juice
thimble full of baking powder
touch of baking soda
thimble full of cinnamon
smidge of nutmeg, allspice & ground cloves
1 stick melted butter
extra mountain honey
¼ jelly jar of moonshine plus another extra ½

I take no responsibility for these measurements if they are right or wrong because Granny never was one to give you all the ingredient amounts in her secret recipes.

I hope ya'll enjoyed this little trip taken with me, reading the recipes and visiting with some of my family members. We do appreciate your company. The recipes are finished and Granny has hidden the little old brown jug somewhere back in the barn where Pappy can't find it. She's leaving the jug there for the next generation so they can make people happy when they commence cooking with its fiery liquid. Now ya'll do realize these recipes can be made with or without alcohol, but where's the fun in that.

I'm going back to the house and kick my flip flops off, stop by the kitchen and make myself a plain old southern glass of sweet ice tea and sit in the cool shade of the parlor. Ah, life sure is grand here in the mountains and the food is extra tasty when ya'll are Cooking Moonshine Style.

Linda June Furr
Author
of
Moonshine Cookin'

## To Order Copies

Please send me _____ copies of *Cookin'
with Moonshine* $9.95 each plus $3.50 for
the first one and $1.50 for each additional
copy for S/H. (Make checks payable to
QUIXOTE **PRESS**.)

Name _____

Street _____

City _____ State _____ Zip _____

**QUIXOTE PRESS**
**3544 Blakslee Street**
**Wever IA   52658**
**1-800-571-2665**

------------------------------------------------

## To Order Copies

Please send me _____ copies of *Cookin'
with Moonshine* $9.95 each plus $3.50 for
the first one and $1.50 for each additional
copy for S/H. (Make checks payable to
QUIXOTE **PRESS**.)

Name _____

Street _____

City _____ State _____ Zip _____

QUIXOTE PRESS
**3544 Blakslee Street**
**Wever IA   52658**
**1-800-571-2665**